£16.99

Including Children with Down's Syndrome in the Early Years Foundation Stage

Written by
Clare Beswick

Illustrated by
Martha Hardy

Published 2009 by A&C Black Publishers Limited
36 Soho Square, London W1D 3QY
www.acblack.com

First published in the UK by Featherstone Education Limited, 2004

ISBN 978-14081-2264-8

Text © Clare Beswick, 2004
Illustrations © Martha Hardy, 2004
Editor, Sally Featherstone

**To see our full range of titles
visit www.acblack.com**

Contents

Introduction   **4**

First steps   **6**

    Making this book work for you   6

    Key facts about Down's syndrome   7

    Successful inclusion   12

    Making the best start   14

    The other side of the fence   15

Down's syndrome and the EYFS framework   **17**

    Personal, social and emotional development   17

    Communication, language and literacy   19

    Problem solving, reasoning and numeracy   21

    Knowledge and understanding of the world   23

    Physical development   25

    Creative development   26

Activities to support learning in the EYFS   **27**

    Personal, social and emotional development   27

    Communication, language and literacy   29

    Problem solving, reasoning and numeracy   31

    Knowledge and understanding of the world   33

    Physical development   35

    Creative development   37

Differentiation and reinforcement   39

Who's who in multi-agency working?   41

Partnership with parents   42

Different approaches   44

Top teaching tips   46

Resources, key contacts and websites   **47**

Introduction

The Early Years Foundation Stage is a great time for all young children. It offers them opportunities to be active learners, to be partners in play, to imagine, create, discover and explore. It allows them to work, develop and progress at their own pace and is ideally suited to promoting the inclusion of all children.

This book can help you make the most of the Early Years Foundation Stage for young children with Down's syndrome. It aims to inform, inspire and reassure you. Early years practitioners are experts in early childhood and have a unique opportunity to really get to know and tune into individual children. The skills, experience and insight you have gained as an early years practitioner are the essential ingredients needed to make inclusion really work for all children in your setting.

Who is this book for?

This book is for anyone with an interest in very young children with Down's syndrome – students and early years practitioners. Many of the practical ideas and suggestions are suitable for all children with developmental delay and can be easily adapted for children of different ages working at this developmental stage.

This book will:

Inform you by:

- providing essential background information about Down's Syndrome;
- signposting you to further resources;
- telling you about the particular learning styles of children with Down's syndrome;
- unravelling the complexities of multi-agency working;
- helping you with different approaches or ways of working.

Support you by:

- giving advice about working with support staff;
- helping you to contribute to a multi-agency team;
- giving practical strategies for differentiation;
- offering tried and tested teaching tips.

Inspire you by:

- giving insight into the parents' perspective;
- suggesting lots of activity ideas across all six areas of learning;
- offering great ideas for making a smooth start.

Make you think by asking:

- How does it feel to have Down's syndrome?

- What's it like to feel different?

- What's it like to parent a child with Down's syndrome?

- What's it like for other family members and close friends?

Make you ask yourself some hard questions such as:

- How can I make this child feel really good about him/herself?

- How can I help other children understand, value and support all children in the setting?

Supporting ideas

Under each of the six areas of learning in the Foundation Stage (pages 27-38) there are lots of suggestions, using everyday resources, that are planned specifically for children with Down's syndrome.

All the pages:

- are packed with easy to do ideas, using everyday resources;

- offer opportunities for small step learning, repetition and reinforcement;

- are linked to the Early Learning Goals in the EYFS framework;

- are planned specifically for children with Down's syndrome, but great for all children starting in the Foundation Stage;

- are written to take careful account of different learning styles and the particular learning styles of children with Down's syndrome.

Making this book work for you

1. Take a little time to read the early pages, background information and ideas for a smooth start.

2. Next, spend time really getting to know the child. Visit them at home so you can listen to their parents and spend time watching and playing alongside them.

3. Read on for more information about what Down's syndrome means for learning. Look at the activity pages, ideas and tips to make sure all the activities planned for children are accessible to the child with special needs.

4. Check out the pages on different approaches and multi-agency working for more information and signposting to further resources.

This book aims to be a practical resource. Keep it handy and dip into it for ideas and inspiration. Pass it round the team so that everyone has an insight into Down's syndrome and what this means for the child as an individual, the other children and the setting as a whole.

Key facts about Down's syndrome

Down's syndrome is one of the most commonly occurring causes of learning difficulty and affects around one in 1000 babies born in the UK. Every child with Down's syndrome is unique but all need extra time and support to enable them to develop to their full potential.

It is important to understand a little about Down's syndrome and the implications for learning so that you can set your knowledge and understanding of each individual child in context to maximise their potential for learning.

Every three, four and five year old in the Foundation Stage has their own interests, learning style and rate of progression.

They have their own strengths and issues, like all of us. Each child with Down's syndrome also has their own interests, learning style and so on, but there are implications of their Down's syndrome for learning, and common features that all children with Down's syndrome share.

Down's syndrome is a genetic condition caused by the presence of an extra chromosome. Every day in the UK, between one and two babies are born with Down's syndrome. All these babies have a learning disability but the level of difficulty varies from individual to individual.

As well as developmental delay, the children have similar physical characteristics. These include:

- an extra fold of skin on their eyelids called an epicanthic fold (this does not affect vision);

- looser muscles and joints that can affect the child's physical development;

- a tendency to be smaller and grow more slowly.

Some children have associated medical conditions that may or may not have implications for their learning. As many as one in three babies with Down's syndrome have heart defects. They may be more susceptible to chest and sinus infections, have difficulties regulating body temperature or have less control of the muscles around the tongue. They are more likely to have a hearing loss.

A specialist paediatrician, or children's doctor, will have seen every baby with Down's syndrome. They are best placed, along with parents, to advise you of the implications of health issues for the individual child in your setting.

The degree of learning difficulty varies widely however, and many children with Down's syndrome grow up to lead long and fulfilled lives. More and more children are successfully included in their local early years provision and go on to the local school, perhaps with additional support.

The success of the inclusion depends upon the attitudes of the staff involved and the resources available to support the child and the staff in adapting the curriculum to ensure that each individual child's learning style and developmental needs are met.

Every child with Down's syndrome is different, but they share common needs:

- they need more individual attention and more early social play with more opportunities to explore and get to know significant people;

- they need more time to watch, think and respond, more stimulation and more motivation;

- they need more time to gain new skills and to have skills broken down into small achievable steps;

- they need lots of opportunities to practise the same skill over and over and to practise the newly learned skill in lots of different situations, with different people, with different objects or toys and so on.

Talking and listening

Becoming a confident and effective communicator, developing understanding of language, acquiring expressive language and using this effectively to communicate with other children and staff (one to one and in small groups) is an essential part of the Early Years Foundation Stage. Children with Down's syndrome need particular help to develop early communication skills, to build their understanding of language and particularly to support the development of their expressive language, which develops more slowly than in other children.

Children with Down's syndrome are often strong visual learners, and need help and support to develop listening skills. They need particular help to develop their auditory discrimination and short-term memory skills. Memory and listening skills are incredibly important for all children, enabling them to become increasingly independent learners.

Poor communication and listening skills will make things more difficult for a child in many situations, but particularly at group times, circle time, listening to stories, in larger groups such as assembly, or when instructions or requests are presented in long strings or without visual clues or prompts.

Playing together

At the beginning of the Early Years Foundation Stage many children are beginning to learn about sharing and turn taking, playing imaginatively, playing alongside or with other children. For children with Down's syndrome, these skills will be starting to emerge, but they will need extra support to get to know and recall the social rules by which we learn together and play. Every child will be different but many will need help to focus their attention, keep them on task and support them in completing activities.

Making it accessible and achievable

Perhaps this is what inclusion really means in practice. There is so much that can be done simply, quickly and without expense to make everyday Early Years Foundation Stage activities accessible and meaningful to children with Down's syndrome. Setting achievable targets, making it interesting and fun and enabling learning to take place alongside other children are the joys and challenges of including children in the Early Years Foundation Stage.

Although each child is different, almost all will be keen to explore and get involved, communicate and make their mark. Carefully planned, small steps will gradually but steadily move a child towards practical and agreed developmental targets. Repetition, real reward and reinforcement will enable the children to retain new skills and build on these to gain further skills.

Take a look at pages 27-38 for ideas to help develop children's skills in all the EYFS six areas of learning.

Remember:

- that all children with Down's syndrome have some degree of learning difficulty, but this can vary widely. Every child is different;

- Down's syndrome will have implications for all six areas of learning;

- to check with parents and medical staff for the implications of any health problems;

- that young children with Down's syndrome are often good visual learners and this can be used to help them develop other skills.

- they will need particular help to become effective communicators.

Find out more about the causes and effects of Down's syndrome from the Down's Syndrome Association. Visit the website at **www.downs-syndrome.org.uk** and download their early years information pack.

What everyone needs to know

Children with Down's syndrome learn more slowly than many other children. As with all children, the rate at which they learn varies from child to child. Much can be done to ensure that they all achieve their potential.

A carefully planned 'small steps' approach is most effective. Each skill to be taught needs to be broken down into small, specific and achievable steps. This ensures success, makes the child feel good about themselves and boosts confidence in everyone.

Each skill needs much practice, with rewards and genuine and meaningful praise. Initially, new skills may need to be taught one-to-one, but also need to be practised in small groups, gradually reducing the support as the skills develop. Lots of practice of the same skill with different resources, in different situations, at home and at nursery will ensure that the skill is retained and extended.

Each child is different and may have associated health issues that can also affect their learning, but most three, four and five year olds with Down's syndrome need particular help with:

- understanding of language;

- expressive language;

- attention and listening skills;

- memory and recall;

- gaining independence with self-help skills.

Most will need help in working towards the earliest 'development matters' guidance for the Early Years Foundation Stage.

Agreeing targets with parents and other professionals involved will ensure that you are all working to a common goal. When choosing targets, consider what is most helpful to the child, in terms of gaining independence, making relationships with the other children and giving them the foundations for further learning.

Successful inclusion

Simple steps

Successful inclusion needs time, flexibility and most importantly a belief that this is the right thing to be doing.

There are many simple steps that you can take to make including a child with Down's syndrome easier and more effective within your setting.

1 Make sure everyone has a clear understanding of what having Down's syndrome means to the child and to the parent. Set aside time to talk this through and plan how everyone can contribute towards successful inclusion.

2 Set aside time for visits and meetings with other professionals involved with the child.

3 Look at your planning and make sure that it meets the needs of all the children and that all activities can be made accessible to the child with Down's syndrome.

4 Plan how the child can practise key skills and work towards targets alongside the other children within day-to-day activities.

5 Organise time and resources for additional individual or very small group work (in twos or threes) to work towards the individual child's agreed targets. Make these a priority.

6 Make sure every member of the team is aware of the child's targets and has the chance to share information.

7 Choose resources carefully and make best use of everyday objects and equipment.

8 Set aside extra time for supporting parents and attending multi-agency meetings.

Tip

Work together!
Shared responsibility is a powerful factor in making inclusion work.

Working together

As an early years practitioner, working together is a natural part of your everyday life. You already work in partnership with parents and other staff, all of whom have different skills, experience, attitudes, roles and responsibilities. You make it work by:

- understanding and respecting each other's roles and responsibilities;
- shared commitment to a common goal;
- being effective communicators;
- making the most of everyone's skills and experience.

Including a child with Down's syndrome is a multi-agency undertaking and involves everyone in nursery and other outside agencies. All the factors listed above, that make your team within the nursery work, are the skills and experience that will enable you to be a confident and effective part of a wider multi-professional team offering support to the child and parent. Take a look at page 41 for 'Who's who in multi-agency working'. Get to know what other professionals involved are providing for the child and family. Ensure that the targets work well together and are fully understood and agreed by all involved.

Tip

Be confident!
Early years practitioners are experts in partnership – you are doing it every day!

Multi-agency working

Multi-agency working takes time, effort and commitment. Plan to share information efficiently and set aside time to prepare for and attend multi-agency meetings. It will be worth the time and effort and is an essential part of good practice. Effective multi-agency working will:

- ensure the child and family get consistent messages;
- mean that approaches blend well together and help the child towards agreed and planned common goals;
- make the most of the wide range of training, skills and experiences of professionals from different sectors;
- make sure everyone is aware of issues of health or development that may have implications for the child and their learning;
- offer the most effective support to parents and children;
- provide additional insight, information and professional development opportunities for all involved.

Making the best start

- Set aside extra time for the home visit. Encourage parents to tell you about their child, what they are hoping for from you, and any concerns.

- Arrange a further home visit for the parents and child to meet the key worker.

- Play with the child's own toys as well as taking something special along to play with from your setting.

- Plan together how the first few days can be made reassuring for their child.

- Find out about the multi-agency team.

- Take a few photographs of your setting for the parents to share with their child.

- Reassure the parents and their child that they can bring their favourite cup, comfort toy or any other special object.

- Explain clearly to the parents what is to be provided for their child and how you will plan and ensure their child's needs are met. Make sure they have the chance to meet the special needs co-ordinator and find out about their role and responsibilities.

- Explain the role of the key person and plan how they can work together.

- Talk about self-help skills and how you can work together towards independence. Talk about how you help children who are not toilet trained, reassuring parents of your commitment, understanding and support.

- Make careful note of any health issues or concerns the parents may have.

- Encourage the child to bring a favourite object or photo from home to show staff and other children. This gives them a great way in and something to share straight away.

and when you get back to your setting...

- Make sure the child's coat peg is easy to reach and find. Why not add a photo of each child to the name card on their peg?

- Make sure that all staff understand any special health or other needs and what they mean for the child and the setting.

- Give the child plenty of time to settle in, but be clear about routines and expectations from the start.

Tip
Remember to listen as well as talk!
Parents may be shy, anxious or worried.

The other side of the fence

Parents need reassurance that their child is welcomed as an equal and valued member of the group. Getting the balance right between allowing them to be just 'one of the crowd' and providing extra reassurance is key.

All this is everyday good practice, but needs more time, more planning and more care for children with Down's syndrome and their families. Starting school or nursery is an exciting and yet daunting prospect for any parent and child, but particularly so for a parent and child with special needs.

Take some time to think about how it might feel to be the parent of a child with Down's syndrome, or indeed to view the world from the child's perspective. This will give you fresh insight and help you to be more effective in providing support to the whole family.

When a baby with Down's syndrome is born, every parent will have different feelings and respond in a different way. The initial reaction may have been shock, or indeed the parents may already have known that their baby would have Down's syndrome. However, almost all new parents of babies with Down's syndrome report initial feelings of shock, anger (Why us? Why my baby?), guilt (Could I have done something to make this happen? – which of course they haven't) and loss. In time, parents usually move gradually towards a feeling of acceptance. Concerns about the future and the effect on other family members and relationships are often most intense. Although these feelings and anxieties may lessen over time, they often increase at times of change, such as starting nursery or school.

All the feelings that any parent has when a child starts to move away from them towards independence are even more real and more intense for the parent of a child with Down's syndrome.

Questions may include:
- How will our child cope?
- Will they have friends?
- How will the other parents be?
- Will they be invited to all the parties?
- What if they have an accident, can't sit still, don't make it to the toilet?
- What if they can't make their needs known?

The list will be endless, and different for each parent! Questions may also include:

- Do they really want my child here?

- Am I a bad parent because I am relieved to be getting a break?

All parents will recognise some or all of these feelings, but for the parent of a child with Down's syndrome, the feelings can be overwhelming at times. Some, of course, may simply take it in their stride. Much will depend on individual personality, personal circumstances, support and the needs of the child.

All this means that the parents may need:

- extra support and preparation around the time their child is starting nursery or school;

- regular positive encouragement and support;

- honest and focused feedback;

- regular contact with the child's key worker;

- just to be one of the mums or dads at the gate.

Tip

Be Patient!
The first stages of the relationship are vital. Take your time, watch, listen and note what happens.

Children with Down's syndrome need to feel safe and secure. They may be emotionally less mature than other three and four year olds and may need more time and support to separate from parents, and to gain confidence and independence in the setting. Having a consistent key worker and a regular routine will do much to ensure that the child settles into the routine. A balance needs to be achieved between ensuring that the child is just alongside the other children, an equal partner in the group, but also has the support and additional attention that they need.

They may need more reminders and guidance to help them understand the rules and routines of your setting. They will be beginning to notice that other children can do some things easily that they take longer to do. This can cause feelings of confusion and anxiety, but as every child in nursery is an individual and their achievements celebrated, much can be done to encourage confidence and self-esteem.

Down's Syndrome and the EYFS Framework

Personal, social and emotional development

Every child with Down's syndrome is different, with different strengths, attitudes, experiences and personality. Despite some common developmental and medical issues, every child is an individual with their own unique likes and dislikes, hopes and ambitions and interests and idiosyncrasies. Like most three and four year olds they are highly sociable beings, keen to get involved in every aspect of their busy lives.

Most three and four year olds with Down's syndrome in the Early Years Foundation Stage will need help to:

- respond to verbal requests and instructions;
- follow the rules in a simple game;
- take turns and cope with sharing;
- follow routines, particularly at group times;
- play co-operatively;
- develop their friendships;
- develop their independence and self help skills.

Some children with Down's syndrome may find some parts of the routine or day more challenging, such as:

- circle time;
- story time;
- imaginative play;
- listening to new stories;
- responding to verbal instructions.

This will be true for many of the youngest or less confident children in your setting, and it is particularly so for a child with Down's syndrome. This may be because of the generalised delay in their development, or more particularly due to their difficulties with verbal instructions, memory and their visual learning style.

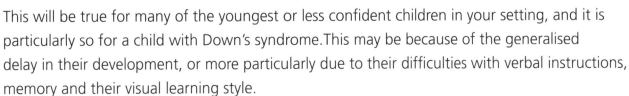

There is so much than can be done working in pairs or very small groups of three children to systematically build the child's confidence and abilities across the learning goals for personal, social and emotional development. Some targets will be very specific, such as gaining independence, self-help or dressing skills, which need to be taught in small incremental steps building towards competency and independence with a very specific skill, such as taking off and hanging up a coat. Others will be more difficult to break down into manageable steps, needing to look at composite skills and experiences for the gradual achievement of these goals.

Everyday objects, simple pretend play around familiar home routines and repetition will provide children working towards or at the earliest PSED developmental stage with a safe framework of activities to build confidence.

The attitude of all the staff and the other children will be important to enabling the child with Down's syndrome to build friendships.

Other children may tend to baby the child with Down's syndrome, rather than see them as an equal partner in their friendships. Sensitive and well timed intervention, knowing when to step back and when to get involved in play, is the key to helping all children negotiate their friendships. Also, it is important to remember that at this developmental stage, many children play independently and spend much time watching other children, before playing alongside or with them.

Structured play in pairs, such as rolling toys back and forth, or turn taking, provides a useful starting point.

On a day-to-day basis, remember to:

- make the most of everyday objects and home corner play;

- try lots of simple turn taking games;

- give the child visual prompts;

- break instructions into small chunks;

- use visual clues to help when negotiating sharing with other children;

- choose very specific and achievable small steps targets with self help skills;

- make routines and expectations very clear and consistent, but always ask yourself if the expectation is realistic and achievable for the child, given what you know of their understanding and developmental stage.

Communication, language and literacy

Most children with Down's syndrome have some speech and language difficulties, although almost all are effective communicators from a very early age, long before spoken language emerges! Many have some degree of fluctuating hearing loss and this also affects the development of language.

Many children may use natural gesture or signing, such as Makaton, to support their expressive language in the early years. The use of signing and natural gesture is very helpful in supporting the development of the understanding of language as well as making sure the child gets the right message across. In this system, signs and speech are used together, and benefit all children in the nursery. As the child's speech becomes clearer and vocabulary grows, many children gradually stop signing as their need for it diminishes.

Few children with Down's syndrome in the Foundation Stage will be able to use language for thinking and reasoning, and will be working towards the earliest stages in the EYFS guidance. Generally, they will use language to label, request and comment on the here and now.

Working on the understanding of language, building expressive language skills, listening skills and memory are priorities for all children in the Foundation Stage, but have even greater significance for children with Down's syndrome.

Most children with Down's syndrome are visual learners who have difficulty with short-term auditory memory. This is the memory we use to hold, process, understand and assimilate spoken language. Short-term memory problems have significant implications for the child's ability to listen and recall, for the way in which they learn to use new words and later, the way they learn to read. Working on memory and listening skills will have great benefits to the child's learning in all areas.

You can make a real difference to a child's working memory by:

- playing listening and memory games;
- providing visual clues and prompts;
- using routines and set sequences in games;
- giving information in small chunks;
- using music, rhyme, rhythm and song;
- making the child aware when they need to stop, focus and listen;
- reducing background and competing noises, to help listening.

Many of the children will already be known to a speech and language therapist, who along with parents will be able to advise about signing and skills that they are working towards. Simple pretend play and many other everyday nursery activities provide the ideal vehicle for developing early language skills, both individually, alongside other children or in small groups of two or three children.

Small steps targets should include:

- building expressive language, including gesture and signing;
- social interaction, such as turn taking and sharing;
- listening skills;
- understanding of language;
- memory and recall.

Watch the child carefully to observe mark making. This is likely to be somewhat delayed. The child will need plenty of encouragement and opportunity for repetition. Their mark making skills will follow the usual sequence of development in young children but will most likely proceed more slowly. Variety is the key, with masses of chances to practise skills at each stage with lots of different and interesting materials. Using a child's special interests or activities of particular significance to them is the best motivator.

When planning activities, consider:

- what motivates and interests the child;
- level of understanding;
- a predominantly visual learning style;
- the ability to listen and attend.

Also plan plenty of rewards, repetitions and activities to reinforce the skills. It is thought that children with Down's syndrome find it easier to respond manually by gesture, signing, pointing, or selecting an object to indicate an answer for tasks, than giving a verbal response. It is important to remember this when observing and assessing the child's developmental stage, as well as when providing support on specific activities.

Books and learning to read

Many children with Down's syndrome have visual processing and memory strengths that enable them to learn to read from a very early age, sometimes from two or three years of age. Learning to recognise written words from such an early age can be a powerful tool in helping the child overcome difficulties with auditory memory. Reading seems to help them build their spoken language and helps them use more sophisticated visual clues and prompts.

See page 47 for further information and resources.

Problem solving, reasoning and numeracy

The early years curriculum guidance for mathematical development includes learning about:

- counting;
- sorting;
- matching;
- patterns;
- making connections;
- numbers, shapes, space and measures;
- using mathematical language and everyday words for mathematical attributes;
- comparing and ordering by length, weight, capacity.

Most children with Down's syndrome will be working towards the earlier stepping stones identified in the curriculum guidance. They will need help and structured support to develop concepts that underpin these earliest steps towards understanding mathematical ideas, including:

- matching objects, colours and pictures;
- matching shapes and textures;
- understanding one, two and three;
- counting to three;
- recognising first numbers and shapes;
- first sorting;
- using everyday words to describe size;
- understanding position, in, on and under.

Each of these early cognitive skills can be achieved using a variety of interesting, rewarding, ordinary activities in a simple, small step by small step approach.

Small steps

For example, to enable children to match pictures in a lotto game, the child first needs to be able to complete these small steps:

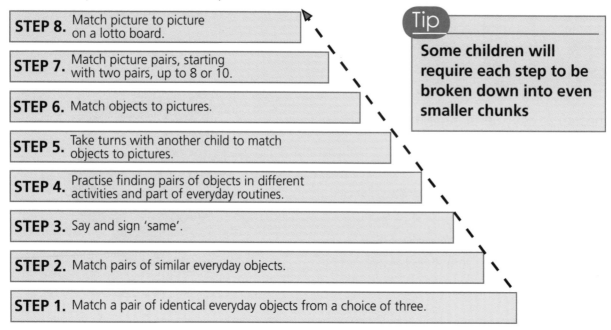

STEP 8. Match picture to picture on a lotto board.

STEP 7. Match picture pairs, starting with two pairs, up to 8 or 10.

STEP 6. Match objects to pictures.

STEP 5. Take turns with another child to match objects to pictures.

STEP 4. Practise finding pairs of objects in different activities and part of everyday routines.

STEP 3. Say and sign 'same'.

STEP 2. Match pairs of similar everyday objects.

STEP 1. Match a pair of identical everyday objects from a choice of three.

> **Tip**
>
> **Some children will require each step to be broken down into even smaller chunks**

Some children will require each step to be broken down into even smaller chunks, such as matching objects to photos of the object, then to very similar pictures, and so on.

To achieve this early mathematical skill, the child will need to put together a range of skills including:

- attention skills;
- turn taking;
- following the rules of a simple game;
- matching;
- visual discrimination skills.

Mathematical skills, language and ideas can be learnt from a range of activities. Planning activities that take account of the preferences and special interests of the child at any one time and include objects of particular significance to the child can be especially useful. Music and rhythm are a great way to help all children to gain mathematical skills.

Children with Down's syndrome need to have as many opportunities as possible to try out each skill and concept, in as many different media as possible. It can be helpful to introduce new ideas and new language in activities that the child finds particularly rewarding.

Careful observation of the child will show you what they already know and give an indication of emerging skills. Using this knowledge will help you to plan activities that are enjoyable and meaningful and will build the child's confidence and competence with mathematical ideas. Many three and four year olds with Down's syndrome enjoy simple pretend play about homes and families. This can be a useful starting point and provide a motivating and real focus for learning. A familiar example might be matching colours of cups, finding a big and little teddy, sorting and stacking plates, finding 'the same' and so on.

Knowledge and understanding of the world

In this area of learning, children develop the skills, knowledge and understanding they need to make sense of the world. They can do this through practical activities and experiences, watching and listening to others, and finding information.

For children at early developmental level who have difficulty processing information presented verbally, like most very young children with Down's syndrome, this area of learning can be made accessible by providing a wide range of stimulating and focused practical activities, centred on everyday situations and experiences that are familiar to them.

As confidence and understanding grows the range of activities can be widened. First, allow plenty of time for children to explore, discover, process and assimilate what they can from experiences based on activities familiar and of particular significance to them.

These should include:

- opportunities to play and explore alongside other children, in very small groups;

- opportunities to play alongside practitioners who can model and guide their discoveries. Adult presence allows the practitioner to provide the language the child needs to label their discoveries, as well as providing essential visual clues and prompts.

- sensory play experiences that allow children to find out about the world using all their senses;

- resources that reflect their general developmental level, such as photo fact books, treasure baskets of everyday objects and so on;

- positive encouragement to try out new ideas and experiences;

- time for simple and repetitive play, for unhurried and uninterrupted discovery.

Many of the 'development matters' in this area of learning and development, require a high level of understanding of language, and the skills to reflect and think, form new ideas, test out theories and so on. Many young children with Down's syndrome understand the world around them in concrete terms in the here and now, and as yet have not developed the ability to plan ahead, report back, investigate and respond to searching questions. However, the child with Down's syndrome can still access many of the activities provided.

Consider whether you could make a difference by:

- adapting the resources;

- providing visual clues and prompts;

- breaking the information down into small chunks;

- presenting the information in a very small group;

- relating the activity back to the child's own individual world and people or objects of particular significance to them.

Using the computer

Using a computer can be a powerful motivator and learning aid for children with Down's syndrome. Many quickly become adept and are highly motivated by the computer.

This may be because a computer:

- presents information visually;

- requires a motor response, rather than speech;

- displays the information for as long as the child needs it;

- provides lots of opportunity for repetition and practice;

- waits for a response without interrupting!

Working alongside other children on the computer gives the child with Down's syndrome a great opportunity to practise social skills and turn taking and to build friendships, as well as work towards targets across all six areas of learning, sometimes with specific software.

Safety tip

Particular attention must be given to safety aspects of activities in this area of learning. The earlier developmental stage of the child with Down's syndrome means that the child may still be exploring by mouthing objects, and will not have an awareness of danger or hazards that you would reasonably expect of other children in the Early Years Foundation Stage.

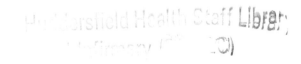

Physical development

Most children with Down's syndrome will have experienced delay in their physical development in the first three years of life. Many have low muscle tone, which means that they may be later to roll over, sit up, stand, crawl (indeed many are bottom shufflers!) and later to walk. Although some children's physical development may have been additionally hampered by medical problems, most children with Down's syndrome will embark on the Early Years Foundation Stage as confident walkers.

'Physical development in the Foundation Stage is about improving skills of co-ordination, control, manipulation and movement.' (DfES Curriculum Guidance for the Foundation Stage). As with most other areas of development, children with Down's syndrome will continue to develop their physical skills and competencies through similar stages of progression to other children with Down's syndrome, although at each stage most of the children will need more steps and more practice.

Again a small steps, structured approach ensures continuity of progress and achievable goals, which will build confidence and sense of well-being, as well as giving positive benefits of an active lifestyle.

As part of the preparation when a child with Down's syndrome starts at your setting, contact with the medical practitioners supporting the child and family will ensure that you are fully aware of any medical or health issues that may have implications for the child's physical development and for particular activities. Regular involvement in multi-agency team meetings will ensure that you are kept up-to-date with any changes.

Careful planning and the selection of achievable small-stepped targets will promote the development of fine motor skills. Children will also need to be encouraged to persevere and persist with tasks, as well as manage and express appropriately any feelings of frustration.

Take care to ensure instructions, support and prompts are presented visually as well as verbally in small chunks, which take account of the child's level of comprehension of language.

Creative development

Creativity is fundamental to who we are, how we explore the world and how we express our feelings and emotions. Creativity enables us to make connections between different experiences and develop our understanding of others, ourselves and our inner world. The child with Down's syndrome will enjoy and benefit as much as any other child from involvement in art, music, dance, role play and imaginative play, and all the activities that contribute to creativity in the Early Years Foundation Stage.

Planning needs to ensure that:

- the children can respond and get involved using a range of senses;

- enough time and space is allowed for the child to take part at their own pace;

- representations involve using a range of materials and equipment, allowing the child with Down's syndrome to play to their strengths;

- there are opportunities to work alone and in very small groups as well as alongside practitioners;

- there is plenty of opportunity for sensory play and discovery;

- activities take account of any sensory impairments. Many children with Down's syndrome have some hearing loss;

- materials used are easy to handle and accessible to all children.

Creative activities offer unique opportunity for social interaction and building friendships. Sensitive support and guidance from the practitioner can help the child with Down's syndrome get involved in a wide range of creative activities, including role play and imaginative play.

Language and thinking skills are essential elements of role and imaginative play, but flexibility and support will enable you to find ways of getting all the children involved. Simple pretend play can be developed into simple role play focused around familiar everyday situations of particular significance to the child with Down's syndrome.

Activities to support learning in the EYFS

Personal, social and emotional development

Early developmental stages

- Develop a curiosity about things and processes
- Have a strong exploratory impulse
- Take pleasure in learning new skills
- Separate from main carer
- Feel safe and secure within healthy relationships with key people
- Relate and make attachments to members of the group
- Seek out others to share experiences
- Begin to accept the needs of others with support
- Show willingness to tackle problems and enjoy self chosen challenges
- Develop confidence in own abilities
- Make connections between different parts of their life experiences

Key skills and attributes

- Anticipation, turn taking and sharing
- Exploring and being curious
- Developing confidence and trust
- Attending and listening
- Being part of a small group
- Understanding routines and expectations

Ideas and activities

- Take turns to add bricks to a tower, rings to a stack, post letters in a box and so on.
- Play lots of 'Ready steady go!' games.
- Practise rolling balls back and forth to each other.
- Try clapping games and 'stacking hands'.

- Model simple pretend play around everyday home routines.
- Put together a scrapbook of photos of the child's family and home to talk about and share.
- Practise imitating and copying actions.
- Offer a treasure basket of everyday objects for free play and talk.
- Practise passing handshakes or objects around a small circle.

Teaching tips

- Keep circle time activities simple, in the here and now and use visual prompts.

- Plan activities that allow the child to respond in a range of ways: verbally, using signing, gesture or pointing, through actions.

- Practise dressing skills every day.

- Give the child a special object to hold or cushion to sit on to help them sit still and attend at story time.

- Give the child plenty of time to be alongside the other children and be an equal partner in activities to enable their friendships to develop.

- Use photographs and picture cards as clues and prompts to help children learn about nursery routines.

- Adapt traditional rhymes and familiar songs to include the name of the child, or to practise key words or skills.

Communication, language and literacy

Early developmental stages

- Communicate in a variety of ways including crying, gurgling, babbling and squealing

- Use single and two word utterances to convey simple messages

- Listen to favourite nursery rhymes, stories and songs. Join in with refrains, anticipating key events and phrases

- Respond to simple instructions

- Listen to others in one to one/small groups when conversation interests them

- Use familiar words to make choices

- Listen to stories with increasing attention and recall

- Use action, sometimes with limited talk, largely concerned with here and now

- Enjoy rhyming and rhythmic activities, distinguish one sound from another

- Listen to and join in with stories and poems, one-to-one and in small groups

- Show interest in illustrations and print in books and in the environment

- Begin to be aware of the way stories are structured

- Draw and paint, sometimes giving meaning to marks

- Engage in activities requiring hand-eye co-ordination

- Use one-handed tools and equipment

Key skills and attributes

- Know names of everyday objects and their use

- Understand and use single words, signs and gestures

- Understand and use two-word phrases to describe possession, e.g. 'mummy's shoe'

- Combine object and action words to make two-word phrases

- Understand and use some simple action words, such as jumping, crying, sleeping

- Identify body parts on self and another

- Listen to a familiar story or rhyme in one-to-one

- Join in with finger play and nursery rhyme actions

- Hold chunky brushes and pens, probably in a palmar grasp to make marks

- Identify pictures, photos and line drawings

- Understand and use big, little, in, on and under

Ideas and activities

- Practise sorting and matching everyday objects, pretending their object use, such as pretending to brush teeth with a toothbrush.
- Try some simple pretend play with a big doll and a small doll, working on understanding of language.
- Use music and rhyme to teach action words, such as 'everybody do this' or 'this is the way we … on a cold and frosty morning'.
- Use mirror play or bathing a doll to work on body part words.
- Trains and cars in, on and under bridges and garages are a great way to find out about prepositions.
- Make small books of photos and signs to look at together.
- Play lots of simple memory games one-to-one and with another child to practise turn taking too.
- Make use of treasure baskets when introducing new words or concepts.
- Provide plenty of opportunity for the child to play alongside another child, such as sharing paper at the easel, taking turns to pour water through a waterwheel or pushing dolls' prams together.

Teaching tips

- Remember many children with Down's syndrome have small hands, so they may find chunky crayons, brushes and felt pens easier.
- Look out for books with photos of everyday objects.
- Learn the Makaton signs for key words in some nursery rhymes and sing and sign with all the children.
- When assessing a child's understanding of language, give opportunity to respond non-verbally, with gesture, pointing, signs or actions.
- Consider using strong visual processing and memory skills to teach reading to help the child with other language skills.
- Make memory games and listening skills a priority.
- Aim for words and phrases that are useful and relevant to the child's everyday life.

Make sure you have the child's attention before giving verbal instructions, so:

- Get down to their level. Use their name first.

Gently touch them on the arm, and keep your hand there, then:

- Use small chunks and short simple phrases.
- Pause to allow the child a few moments to process the information, then repeat.
- Consistently use signs and natural gesture alongside words.

Problem solving, reasoning and numeracy

Early developmental stages

- Show an interest in numbers and counting

- Use some number language, such as 'more' and 'a lot'

- Enjoy joining in with number rhymes and songs

- Say some counting words randomly

- Compare two groups of objects saying when they have the same number

- Show an interest in shape and space by playing with shapes or making arrangements with objects

- Show an awareness of similarities in shapes in the environment

- Observe and use positional language

- Use size language such as 'big' and 'little'

Key skills and attributes

- Matching and sorting objects, pictures and shapes

- Putting objects in and out of a container, pieces in and out of an inset puzzle or form board, and pegboard

- Using number words, one, two, three

- Joining in with number rhymes and finger play

- Understanding and using 'big' and 'little'

- Ordering objects by size

- Understanding signs and saying 'same' and 'different'

- Look out for three-piece shape sorters, or make a single shape sorter from a shoe box and a single shape.
- Practise stacking bricks and beakers, putting rings on stacks and nesting beakers.
- Learn 'big' and 'little' using everyday objects such as a collection of socks and gloves.
- Try sorting everyday objects and toy objects.
- Play pairs games with shapes.
- Make a simple posting box and take turns to post named cards, identifying colours and shapes.
- Make up some very short 1, 2, 3 counting rhymes, such as '1, 2, 3, clap with me', or '1, 2, 3, yum, yum yum, 1, 2, 3, milk in my tum'.
- Spend plenty of time, feeling shapes, looking for simple easy to reach shapes in the environment. Why not put together a collection of round objects in a basket for them to explore?
- Learn the signs for colours and reinforce these through song and everyday use. Why not all learn to sing and sign 'My big blue boat has two red sails' and other colour rhymes?

Teaching tips

- Use real everyday objects as much as possible.
- Use all the senses and lots of different activities to teach mathematical language.
- Use music and song to reinforce ideas and mathematical language.
- Introduce new words and concepts one at a time.
- Use a child's favourite activities, such as water play, to introduce mathematical ideas or language, or to practise counting to three.
- Use a small step structured approach to build skills and understanding, with lots of practise with a wide range of activities.

Knowledge and understanding of the world

Early developmental stages

- Show curiosity and interest by facial expression, movement and sound

- Use movement and senses to focus on, reach for and handle objects

- Describe simple features of objects and events

- Explore objects and materials

- Are curious and interested in making things happen

- Investigate construction materials

- Realise tools can be used for a purpose

- Show an interest in ICT

- Remember and talk about significant things that have happened to them

- Show an interest in the world in which they live

Key skills and attributes

- Confidence to explore and discover

- Be curious, motivated and interested

- Attention and task completion skills

- Understand, use and sign describing words and short phrases

- Fine motor skills to handle and build with simple construction toys

- Understand and use words and signs to describe feelings

Ideas and activities

- Provide lots of opportunity for sensory play

- Look out for easy to handle construction toys, chunky bricks, stickle bricks or magnetic building blocks

- Make the most of the PC, providing lots of opportunity to practise skills; many children with Down's syndrome enjoy and progress quickly with computer skills, perhaps due to their visual learning style and the chance to respond with actions instead of words

- Telephone play gives the child a chance to explore ICT as well as practise communication skills

- Use pictures and photographs to prompt talk about home and family. Make a treasure bag or use a simple drawstring bag for the child to bring objects to share and talk about with you to and from home.

- Look out for pictures and photographs that show different emotions and feelings. These will help when you are learning to say and sign the words to describe feelings.

- Plan for simple pretend play around everyday routines, such as washing up, bathing dolls, shopping, cooking and so on.

Teaching tips

- Use visual prompts and clues to provide instructions, ideas and inspiration.
- Make the most of sensory play and treasure basket play.
- Sing simple commentaries to emphasise key words or encourage repetition.
- Plan for extra time, to take things more slowly, to explore new and familiar objects using all the senses.

Physical development

Early developmental stages

- Move spontaneously in available space

- Respond to rhythm, music and story by means of gesture and movement

- Move in a range of ways, such as shuffling, rolling, jumping, skipping, sliding and hopping

- Use body control to create intended movements, combine and repeat a range of movements

- Negotiate an appropriate pathway when walking or running both indoors and out

- Can stop

- Judge body space in relation to spaces available when fitting into confined spaces

- Show awareness of a range of healthy practices with regard to eating, sleeping and hygiene

- Begin to make and manipulate objects and tools

Key skills and attributes

- Be mobile and keen to explore

- Listen to and understand short phrases and instructions

- Imitate actions

- Follow simple rules

- Walk or run and stop, and change direction

- Be active safely alongside other children

- Understand and use signs and words to describe how they feel, such as hungry, thirsty, tired

- Use an effective grip to manipulate small objects

- Transfer objects from one hand to another, drop and pick up small objects

- Move safely from sitting to standing, standing to sitting, manage steps safely

- Try lots of rolling and throwing and target type play. Try rolled up socks, small soft balls and beach balls. Encourage two hands together when appropriate such as with quoits, balls and so on.

- Encourage the child to try trundle trucks and small trikes, pushing and pulling prams and trolleys.

- Use simple pull-along toys. Attach a string to a shoe box and pull teddy along.

- Make up little songs and rhymes or sing commentaries to encourage children to practise ducking under, stopping, climbing safely and so on, such as for steps 'Up we go, slowly slowly, head up, hold on tight'.

- Use photos and everyday situations to teach words and signs to describe feelings.

Teaching tips

- Check out with parents and medical professionals involved if the child has any difficulties regulating their body temperature, or any other health issues and if this has any implications for active play in your setting.

- Children with Down's syndrome often have a degree of hypotonia, or low muscle tone. They tend to have been floppy babies who needed extra encouragement and exercises to help them with their physical development and to achieve physical milestones, such as sitting or standing. They may still be physically less confident than other children and may have had less experience of active play. With encouragement and the company of other children, they quickly gain confidence and become keen to get involved in active play.

- They also tend to have small hands so look for easy to grip pens and brushes. Make handles chunkier and easier to grip by wrapping tape around them.

- Try 'squeeze scissors' and encourage the child to snip at the paper.

- A non-slip mat is great for keeping paper and puzzles still.

- Use routines and picture prompts to help children learn how to go about tasks safely.

Creative development

Early developmental stages

- Create and experiment with blocks, colour and marks

- Explore colour, texture, shape, form and space in two or three dimensions

- Make three dimensional structures

- Join in favourite songs

- Show an interest in the way musical instruments sound

- Respond to sound with body movement

- Enjoy joining in with dancing and ring games

- Pretend that one object represents another, especially when objects have characteristics in common

- Imitate and create movement in response to music

- Seek to make sense of what they see, hear, smell, touch and feel

- Use language and other forms of communication to share the things they create, or to indicate personal satifaction or frustration

Key skills and attributes

- Curiosity and confidence to explore and express themselves

- Imitate actions

- Use all their senses to explore

- Express emotions and feelings, using words and, non-verbally, through signs and actions

- Listening and attending

- Be part of a small group and follow simple rules

Ideas and activities

- Use simple everyday situations such as a windy day, puddles, or routines at home as starting points for activities. This will help the child to make connections between different parts of their life.

- Provide lots of opportunity for sensory play and discovery.

- Make a collection of simple sound makers or improvised instruments. Use these in listening and memory games and to practise turn taking and imitating. Try copying patterns of sound, taking turns with sounds and making new sounds. Hide a ticking clock and hunt for it together.

- Try using preferred activities, such as the computer, as a means of creative expression. Many children with Down's syndrome will prefer the visual presentation of information and the unhurried, uninterrupted opportunity to process and assimilate information.

Teaching tips

- Use music and rhythm as a vehicle for expressing emotions as well as for teaching skills across all six areas of learning.

- Try very small groups of two or three children for new creative activities.

- Give verbal instructions in small chunks, with visual clues and prompts.

Differentiation and reinforcement

Understanding differentiation

Throughout the Early Years Foundation Stage, each child will progress at their own pace, and each will have their own unique interests and learning styles. This is, of course, also true for children with Down's syndrome. Generally, children with Down's syndrome learn most effectively when activities are presented visually, when signs and gesture are used alongside spoken language, and when instructions are broken down into small chunks. They also (like all young children) learn best from doing, from activities focused on everyday situations and routines of particular importance to them.

Children can be taught in different ways. This is referred to as 'differentiation'. Differentiation ensures that teaching is most effective and the child makes the best possible progress.

Differentiation is a continuous process, changing in response to the changing needs of the child. It involves:

- recognising individual needs and learning styles;
- ensuring planned activities are accessible and supplemented by additional support, so they are most effective in meeting the needs of the child;
- observing, assessing and planning for each indivdual;
- recording and evaluating.

Differentiation in the Early Years Foundation Stage happens in the following ways:

- Differentiation by the resources used
  This could be using different toys, equipment or materials to make the activity accessible to the child, such as using a chunky threading string for a threading activity, providing photograph picture books and so on.

- Differentiation by the activity provided
  This could be by providing a different but related task, such as matching pairs of everyday objects, instead of matching picture pairs, or a lotto picture game.

- Differentiation by group size
  This will depend upon the activity and the child's needs.

- Differentiation by the way information is presented

  This is about matching the way instructions and information are provided to the understanding, attention and listening skills and learning style of the child. It could also involve using clues and prompts, real concrete objects or other visual prompts such as pictures, signs or symbols.

- Differentiation by the support provided

  This is about matching the sort of support provided to the needs of the child at that moment. It may be a practitioner working alongside the child and all the different levels of intervention or guidance that this implies, it may be support from another child, it may be the prompts, or indeed any other sort of support as appropriate to the child's needs.

- Differentiation by the response or outcome expected

  This could be the child making a pointing gesture rather than verbal response, listening or attending for a different length of time on a particular activity and so on.

Understanding reinforcement

The small step, structured approach, using prompts to support learning, provides plenty of opportunity to reinforce skills previously learnt. Children need to have opportunity to:

- practise emerging skills often;

- have a chance to use these skills one-to-one and in small groups;

- blend newly learnt skills with existing skills, such as having learnt to match pictures, the child needs to learn to take turns with another child, (a previously learnt skill), to match the pictures, building towards playing a small lotto game;

- to have time and opportunity to assimilate their learning and use it spontaneously, in different situations, with different people, or independently.

Early years settings are ideally positioned for this, as there are plenty of chances to practise emerging skills as they provide:

- a wide range of different activities;

- a flexible approach;

- hands on learning;

- different group sizes ;

- opportunity to use all the senses;

- activities using everyday objects and routines.

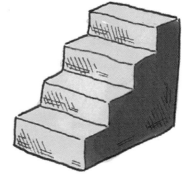

Considering differentiation and strategies for reinforcing emerging skills and learning is absolutely essential and will make all the difference to everyone involved.

Who's who in multi-agency working?

Speech and language therapist

Working often from a community health centre, specialist centre or from a child development centre at a hospital, speech and language therapists offer advice and therapy to build communication skills,including signing. Therapy may be direct one-to-one, or small group work, or maybe in the form of advice and support to parents, again either individually or at a group.

Educational psychologist

Responsible for offering advice and support to schools and for assessing the learning needs of children.

Health visitor

Often working in conjunction with the child's family doctor, providing health advice and support to all parents of babies and young children.

Physiotherapist

Working to encourage babies and young children's physical development, focusing on gross motor skills and, for children with Down's syndrome, providing exercises to help babies and young children overcome the low muscle tone, or hypotonia often associated with Down's syndrome.

Specialist health visitor

Provides health visitor support to parents of babies and young children with special needs.

Specialist pre-school teaching support or Portage worker

Specialist early years practitioners providing structured learning for babies and young children, often one-to-one in the child's home, and providing advice and support to parents.

You may also meet...

Social services professionals, Home Start volunteers, occupational therapists, and (if the child has a sensory impairment) there may be other specialist teachers. The team may also include parent partnership workers or independent parental support workers.

and of course there will be...

Early Years practitioners: setting managers, key persons, a range of different practitioners, and the special needs co-ordinator (SENCO) who ensures the child has the best possible support from the team and an Individual Education or Learning Plan (IEP).

Partnership with parents

Pages 15 and 16 will have given you some insight into what it might feel like to be the parent of a young child with Down's syndrome. Establishing a good relationship with the parents will bring benefits to you and to them, and ultimately to the child. There is much you (and the parents too) can do to help establish a rapport:

- Make the time to listen to each other.

- Tune into their mood.

- Start and finish on a positive note.

- Ask their opinion.

- Try not to interrupt or say you know just how they feel.

- Let them know how much you enjoy working with their child.

- Find out what they want to know. Some parents particularly want to know what their child has had to eat or drink, what they have being doing, or who they are playing with. Ask them what they need to know.

- Get the message across that you see their child as an individual, not a child with Down's syndrome.

- Mention what you have observed, such as 'I noticed that when I used the chunky pens she stayed much longer at the drawing table'.

- Give real positive messages, such as '*name* is really starting to understand some action words'. Go on to describe the activity and be specific in your feedback.

- Encourage them to bring in objects and photos from home. Where possible, let them take home particularly helpful resources to borrow, or visit the local toy library together.

- Take account of their priorities when setting targets.

- Work together on planning targets related to self-help skills.

- Be reassuring about meeting their child's toilet needs.

More ideas

- Put together a photo album of key objects and most significant people and favourite toys and activities to share between home and your setting.

- Make a safe place for the child to put special toys or objects they need to bring from home. Make sure both parent and child know it will be safe, but accessible.

- Ask about the rest of the family, such as 'How is *name* with the baby?', or 'What does *name* like doing with his big sister?'

- Talk about what is happening to make inclusion work, such as practical examples of differentiation.

- Ask if you may observe a session when the speech and language therapist, or specialist pre-school teacher is working with the child, so that you can all make sure that you are working together most effectively.

- Make sure the parent has a copy of their child's individual education plan and the targets across all areas of learning.

- If a parent is working or has little time available when they collect their child, do make other arrangements to meet informally to talk, discuss progress and listen to their concerns and aspirations for their child. A home–school diary sheet may help but is no substitute for getting together in person.

Different approaches

In this book, the focus has been on a small steps structured approach to teaching new skills, differentiating the early years curriculum and providing opportunity to practise and reinforce emerging skills. This approach may be supplemented by different approaches, often suggested by parents or other professionals working with the child and family. Read on for a brief introduction to each approach, and details of how to find out more.

Makaton

Makaton is a structured language programme for the teaching of communication, language and literacy skills. It is specifically devised for children and adults with a variety of communication and learning disabilities and is often used to support the early language development of children with Down's syndrome.

Makaton involves using signs, as well as gesture, facial expression and eye contact, alongside the word. Symbols are also sometimes used, particularly if the child has additional difficulties, perhaps with physical skills, which may make signing difficult. Makaton helps the development of understanding of language as well as spoken language. Research shows that signs and gestures are easier to learn than spoken words and that the use of Makaton does not delay the use of spoken language.

If a child is going to learn to understand and use signs then they need to see others using signs themselves. Everybody needs to get involved. An easy way to start using signs in your setting is to introduce signs around routines, such as milk at drinks time, book at story time, or by signing as well as singing nursery rhymes.

Find out more about Makaton from your local speech and language therapy service and from the Makaton Vocabulary Development Project (contact details on page 47).

Signalong

This is a signing system developed in the 1980's to help people with language difficulties associated with learning difficulties develop their communication skills. Signalong is based on British Sign Language and is designed to complement structured language learning schemes, such as the Derbyshire Language Scheme and Living Language.

Signalong has a wide vocabulary of signs and some excellent support materials, including some for the early years.

Find out more from your speech and language therapy service or from Signalong, (contact details on page 47).

Teaching reading

Given time, many children with Down's syndrome can learn to read to a level that will have practical benefits for them and will have a positive effect in the development of their spoken language.

From as young as two years of age, many children can use their visual skill strengths to learn to recognise written words. This can really help the development of their spoken language. Teaching reading helps because the print makes language visual, helping the child to overcome the difficulty in learning through listening. The print can be looked at for as long as needed for the child to process and remember it, helping with the memory difficulties experienced by many children with Down's syndrome.

Reading can also be used to help improve the child's understanding of language. Research suggests that the most effective way to teach reading to very young children with Down's syndrome is using a small steps structured approach teaching individual words using a 'match, select and name' process. Find out more from the Down Syndrome Information Network (contact details on page 47) where you can read online or purchase 'Meeting the Educational Needs of Children with Down Syndrome; A Handbook for Teachers' by Sue Buckley and Gillian Bird (Portsmouth University Press).

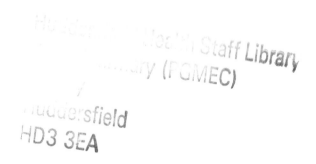

Top teaching tips

Ten top tips for supporting children with Down's syndrome:

1. Present information with visual clues.

2. Use a small steps structured approach.

3. Give verbal information in small chunks.

4. Allow uninterrupted time for the child to process what they have heard.

5. Plan for the child to be able to respond non verbally.

6. Encourage pointing, gesture and signing, alongside spoken language.

7. Use everyday objects and situations significant to the child.

8. Think about the child's understanding of language, visual learning strengths and memory difficulties when planning differentiation.

9. Make language and self-help skills a priority.

10. Have fun together, laughter is a great positive reward.

Resources, key contacts and websites

Down's Syndrome Association
155 Mitcham Road Tooting, London SW17 9PG
Tel: 0845 230 0372
Fax: 020 8682 4012
Email: info@downs-syndrome.org.uk
www.downs-syndrome.org.uk

Down Syndrome Educational Trust
The Sarah Duffen Centre, Belmont Street,
Southsea, Hants PO5 1NA
Tel: 0123 9285 5330
Fax: 0123 9285 5320
Email: enquiries@downsed.org
www.downsed.org

For your bookshelf

SEN Code of Practice
on the Identification and Assessment of Pupils
with Special Educational Needs
DCSF

Let Me Speak
Dorothy Jeffre and Roy McConkey
Souvenir Press 1995
ISBN 0285648284

Let Me Play
Dorothy Jeffre, Roy McConkey;
Simon Hewson
Souvenir Press 1994
ISBN 0285648357

**Early Support Developmental Journal
for babies and children with Downs
Syndrome** DCSF

On the web

Early Support Programme
www.earlysupport.org.uk
Government programme for co-ordination of information and services, includes a
developmental journal for babies and children with Down's Syndrome

Makaton Development Project
www.makaton.org
More information for parents and practitioners; advice about training

Down's Syndrome Association
www.downs-syndrome.org.uk
Masses of information, including a free to download information pack for early years
practitioners

Down's Information Network
www.down-syndrome.org/
Comprehensive range of resources and services, including an easy to use free online library

Signalong
www.signalong.org.uk
More information and support materials

Down Syndrome Educational Trust
www.downsed.org
Information, books, training and dvd entitled 'Down Syndrome in Practice' – activities for
babies (birth to around 18 months)

Other titles in this series

Including Children with:

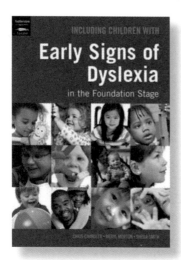

Dyslexia
by Chris Chandler,
Meryl Morton and
Sheila Smith
9781904187905

Asperger's Syndrome
by Clare Beswick

9781905019113

Autistic Spectrum
Disorders (ASD)
by Clare Beswick
9781904187288

Attention and
Behaviour
Difficulties (ABD)
by Maureen Garner
9781905019014

Working Within
the P Levels
by Kay Holman and
Janet Beckett
9781905019380

Developmental
Co-ordination
Disorder (Dyspraxia)
by Sharon Drew
9781905019458

All available from www.acblack.com/featherstone